THE PSYCHOLOGY OF SPARRING

01 FACING FEAR:
AN INTRODUCTION TO SPARRING ANXIETY — 1-9

02 THE FIGHT OR FLIGHT RESPONSE:
UNDERSTANDING YOUR BODY'S REACTIONS — 10-15

03 ADRENALINE:
FRIEND OR FOE? — 16-21

04 THE MIND-BODY CONNECTION:
HARNESSING MENTAL STRENGTH — 22-26

05 BUILDING CONFIDENCE:
THE FIRST STEPS IN TAEKWON-DO — 27-31

06 TECHNIQUES TO TAME ANXIETY:
PRACTICAL EXERCISES — 32-36

07 SPARRING AS SELF-DEFENCE:
REAL-WORLD APPLICATIONS — 37-41

08 FROM THE DOJANG TO DAILY LIFE:
APPLYING LESSONS BEYOND SPARRING — 42-46

09 OVERCOMING SOCIAL ANXIETY:
A PERSONAL JOURNEY IN TAEKWON-DO — 47-52

10 THE PATH FORWARD:
EMBRACING THE CHALLENGE OF SPARRING — 53-57

CHAPTER 01

FACING FEAR

INTRODUCTION TO SPARRING ANXIETY

Fear is a universal emotion, intrinsic to the human experience. From the earliest days of our species, fear has been a critical survival mechanism, alerting us to danger and prompting us to take action. In the modern world, while we are less likely to encounter predators, fear manifests in various forms, impacting our thoughts, behaviors, and decisions. For many individuals, the fear of sparring in martial arts represents a significant psychological barrier. This chapter delves into the nature of this fear, the underlying mechanisms, and the first steps toward overcoming it.

Martial arts, regardless of the specific discipline, require a balance of physical skill and mental fortitude. Whether it's Taekwon-Do, Karate, Judo, or any other form, sparring is an integral part of the training. Sparring involves facing an opponent in a controlled combat scenario, testing both your physical abilities and your mental resilience. For many, the idea of sparring can evoke intense anxiety and fear, which can be a major hurdle to progress in martial arts training.

Understanding the nature of sparring anxiety begins with recognising the psychological and physiological responses to fear. When faced with a perceived threat, our bodies activate the fight-or-flight response. This ancient survival mechanism prepares us to either confront the danger or flee from it. In the context of sparring, the threat is not life-threatening, but our bodies and minds often react as if it is. The rush of adrenaline, increased heart rate, and heightened alertness are all part of this response.

The fear of sparring can stem from various sources. For some, it is the fear of physical harm or injury. For others, it is the fear of failure or embarrassment. The prospect of facing an opponent, especially in front of peers or instructors, can be intimidating. Additionally, the unpredictability of sparring, where the outcome is uncertain and the opponent's actions are not fully known, can amplify this fear.

Overcoming sparring anxiety is a gradual process, and it begins with acknowledging the fear. It is important to understand that feeling anxious or scared before sparring is normal and experienced by practitioners at all levels. Recognising this commonality can help reduce the sense of isolation and self-judgment that often accompanies fear.

One of the first steps in addressing sparring anxiety is to break down the fear into manageable parts. Start by focusing on what you can control, such as your breathing, posture, and mindset. Deep breathing exercises can help calm the nervous system and reduce the physical symptoms of anxiety. Visualization techniques, where you mentally rehearse sparring scenarios and positive outcomes, can also be effective in building confidence and reducing fear.

Additionally, gradual exposure to sparring can help desensitize you to the fear. Begin with light, controlled sparring sessions with a trusted partner or instructor. As you become more comfortable, gradually increase the intensity and unpredictability of the sparring sessions. This step-by-step approach allows you to build confidence and resilience over time.

Another important aspect of overcoming sparring anxiety is to shift your mindset. Instead of viewing sparring as a test or a competition, try to see it as an opportunity for growth and learning. Embrace the mistakes and setbacks as part of the learning process. Every sparring session, regardless of the outcome, provides valuable lessons that can help you improve.

Building a supportive environment is also crucial. Surround yourself with instructors and peers who understand your fears and are willing to support you. Positive reinforcement and constructive feedback can boost your confidence and motivation. Additionally, finding a training partner who shares similar anxieties can create a sense of camaraderie and mutual support.

Ultimately, the journey to overcoming sparring anxiety is deeply personal and varies for each individual. For me, martial arts became a powerful tool to confront and manage my social anxiety. The structure, discipline, and community within the dojang provided a safe space to face my fears. Through consistent practice and gradual exposure, I learned to channel my anxiety into focus and determination.

Sparring in martial arts is not just about physical combat; it is a mental and emotional challenge that can lead to profound personal growth. By facing your fears in the controlled environment of a martial arts training session, you can build resilience, confidence, and mental strength that extend beyond the dojo. This journey is not easy, but it is immensely rewarding. Through persistence, support, and a willingness to embrace the challenge, you can overcome your sparring anxiety and unlock new levels of potential in both your martial arts practice and your life.

UNDERSTANDING FEAR

THE PRIMAL EMOTION

To address sparring anxiety, we must first understand what fear is and how it operates within our bodies and minds. Fear is an emotional response to perceived threats, characterised by heightened arousal, a rush of adrenaline, and a cascade of physiological reactions. When we perceive danger, our bodies enter a state of heightened readiness, commonly known as the "fight-or-flight" response. This response, governed by the sympathetic nervous system, prepares us to either confront the threat or escape from it.

In the context of sparring, fear can be triggered by various factors: the anticipation of pain, the fear of failure or embarrassment, and the anxiety of performing under pressure. The dojang, or training hall, becomes an arena where these fears come to the forefront, challenging practitioners to confront their deepest insecurities.

The Anatomy of Sparring Anxiety

Sparring anxiety is a multifaceted phenomenon, encompassing physical, psychological, and social dimensions. It is essential to dissect these components to develop a comprehensive strategy for managing and overcoming this anxiety.

- **PHYSICAL REACTIONS**

    The physical symptoms of sparring anxiety can be intense and overwhelming. Common reactions include increased heart rate, rapid breathing, sweating, trembling, and muscle tension. These symptoms are the result of adrenaline flooding the bloodstream, preparing the body for action. While these reactions are natural, they can be debilitating if not managed effectively.

- **PSYCHOLOGICAL FACTORS**

    The mental aspect of sparring anxiety is equally complex. Negative thoughts, self-doubt, and catastrophic thinking can dominate the mind, undermining confidence and performance. The fear of getting hurt, making mistakes, or losing can create a mental block preventing individuals from fully engaging in sparring practice.

- **SOCIAL INFLUENCES**

    The social environment of the dojang can also contribute to sparring anxiety. The presence of peers, instructors, and spectators can heighten the pressure to perform well. The fear of judgement or criticism can amplify anxiety, making it difficult to focus on the task at hand.

PERSONAL REFLECTIONS

MY JOURNEY WITH SPARRING ANXIETY

From a young age, I struggled in social situations, to a level where it took over my life. One day, I decided to tackle this. I decided to look for a Karate school but rang a Taekwon-Do school instead. This didn't matter too much to me, I just knew this was a very difficult arena for me to be in, and so therefore I was prepared to do it.

My journey with Taekwon-Do began as a means to cope with severe social anxiety. Walking into the dojang for the first time was a daunting experience. I remember the flood of emotions – excitement, curiosity, but most of all, fear. The thought of sparring, of facing an opponent in a controlled combat scenario, was terrifying. However, I soon realised that this fear was not unique to me. Many of my fellow practitioners, regardless of their skill level, experienced similar anxieties.

I vividly recall my first sparring session. My heart raced, my palms were sweaty, and I could barely focus on the instructions. As I faced my opponent, a fellow beginner, I felt exposed and vulnerable. The first few exchanges were clumsy, and I made countless mistakes. But with each session, I began to see a shift in my mindset.

Taekwon-Do became more than just a physical activity; it turned into a mental training ground. Every time I stepped onto the mat, I was confronted with my fears. The controlled environment of the dojang allowed me to face these fears in a structured and supportive setting. I learned to manage my anxiety by focusing on my breathing, grounding myself in the moment, and trusting in the techniques I was being taught.

The discipline and routine of Taekwon-Do provided a sense of stability in my life. The rituals of bowing, warming up, and practising patterns became a comforting constant. Sparring, with all its intensity, became a metaphor for the struggles I faced in everyday life. Each match taught me valuable lessons about resilience, patience, and self-control.

There were many days when my anxiety felt overwhelming, and I considered quitting. I also found that the physical exertion of Taekwon-Do helped to alleviate my anxiety. The rigorous training sessions left me physically tired but mentally clear. The endorphins released during intense workouts provided a natural antidote to the stress and worry that often clouded my mind. Over time, I noticed that I was not just becoming stronger and more skilled in Taekwon-Do, but I was also becoming more confident and less anxious in social situations.

As I progressed through the ranks, the challenges became more complex, but so did my coping strategies. Advanced techniques and more intense sparring sessions required greater focus and mental fortitude. I learned to channel my anxiety into energy and determination. Each belt promotion was a testament to my growing self-belief and my ability to face and overcome my fears.

My journey with Taekwon-Do has been transformative. It has taught me that fear and anxiety are not insurmountable obstacles but challenges that can be managed and overcome. Sparring, in particular, has shown me the importance of confronting my fears head-on. It has helped me to build resilience, develop mental strength, and cultivate a sense of inner peace.

Today, I still experience anxiety, but it no longer controls my life to the same degree. Taekwon-Do has given me the tools to face my fears with courage and confidence. It has become a vital part of my mental health toolkit, helping me to navigate the complexities of life with greater ease. My journey with sparring anxiety is ongoing, but I now face it with a sense of empowerment and hope.

Through this book, I hope to share the lessons I have learned and inspire others to find their own paths to overcoming fear and anxiety. Taekwon-Do has been a lifeline for me, and I believe it can be for others as well. Whether you are a seasoned martial artist or a complete beginner, I encourage you to embrace the challenge of sparring and discover the strength within yourself.

The Fight-or-Flight Response: A Closer Look

To manage sparring anxiety, it is crucial to understand the fight-or-flight response and how it affects our bodies and minds. This response is an automatic reaction to perceived threats, designed to enhance our chances of survival. When faced with danger, the brain sends signals to the adrenal glands, prompting the release of adrenaline and other stress hormones. These hormones trigger a series of physiological changes:

- **INCREASED HEART RATE**

    The heart pumps faster to supply muscles with more oxygen and energy.

- **RAPID BREATHING**

    The respiratory rate increases to take in more oxygen, which is then transported to vital organs and muscles.

- **MUSCLE TENSION**

    Muscles become tense and ready for action, improving strength and speed.

- **HEIGHTENED SENSES**

    Vision, hearing, and other senses become more acute, helping to detect and respond to threats.

While these changes are beneficial in genuine life-threatening situations, they can be counterproductive in a controlled sparring environment. The key to overcoming sparring anxiety lies in learning how to regulate the fight-or-flight response, using techniques that calm the mind and body.

Techniques for Managing Sparring Anxiety

Managing sparring anxiety requires a multifaceted approach, incorporating physical, mental, and emotional strategies. Here are some effective techniques to help you face your fears and improve your sparring performance:

- **BREATHING EXERCISES**

    Controlled breathing is a powerful tool for managing anxiety. Techniques such as diaphragmatic breathing, box breathing, and the 4-7-8 method can help calm the nervous system and reduce the physical symptoms of anxiety. Practising these exercises regularly can enhance your ability to stay composed during sparring sessions.

- **VISUALISATION**

    Mental imagery can be a valuable technique for reducing anxiety and building confidence. Visualise yourself sparring with ease, executing techniques flawlessly, and handling challenges with poise. By creating positive mental scenarios, you can condition your mind to respond more effectively in real sparring situations.

- **PROGRESSIVE MUSCLE RELAXATION**

    This technique involves systematically tensing and relaxing different muscle groups to reduce overall tension and promote relaxation. Practising progressive muscle relaxation can help you become more aware of your body's stress responses and learn how to release tension before and during sparring.

- **POSITIVE SELF-TALK**

    Replacing negative thoughts with positive affirmations can significantly impact your mindset. Develop a set of encouraging statements, such as "I am capable," "I am prepared," and "I can handle this." Repeat these affirmations regularly to build selfconfidence and counteract anxiety.

- **GRADUAL EXPOSURE**

    Gradual exposure to sparring can help desensitise you to the fear and anxiety associated with it. Start with light, controlled sparring sessions and gradually increase the intensity and complexity of the matches. This approach allows you to build confidence and skills progressively, reducing anxiety over time.

- **MINDFULLNESS AND MEDITATION**

    Practising mindfulness and meditation can help you stay present and focused during sparring. Mindfulness involves paying attention to the present moment without judgement, while meditation can help calm the mind and reduce stress.

BUILDING CONFIDENCE

THE FOUNDATION OF EFFECTIVE SPARRING

Confidence is a crucial element in overcoming sparring anxiety. Building confidence requires consistent practice, positive reinforcement, and a supportive environment. Here are some strategies to help you develop confidence in your sparring abilities:

- **SET REALISTIC GOALS**

    Establishing achievable goals can provide a sense of direction and purpose in your training. Break down larger objectives into smaller, manageable steps, and celebrate your progress along the way. Setting and achieving goals can boost your confidence and motivation.

- **PRACTISE REGULARLY**

    Consistent practice is essential for skill development and confidence building. Regular training sessions allow you to refine your techniques, improve your physical conditioning, and become more comfortable with sparring. The more you practise, the more confident you will become in your abilities.

- **SEEK FEEDBACK AND SUPPORT**

    Constructive feedback from instructors and peers can help you identify areas for improvement and reinforce your strengths. Surround yourself with supportive individuals who encourage and motivate you. Positive reinforcement from others can significantly enhance your confidence and self-esteem.

- **EMBRACE CHALLENGES**

    View sparring challenges as opportunities for growth rather than threats. Embrace the learning process, and don't be afraid to make mistakes. Each sparring session is a chance to learn, adapt, and improve. By adopting a growth mindset, you can build resilience and confidence.

- **REFLECT ON PROGRESS**

    Take time to reflect on your progress and acknowledge your achievements. Keep a training journal to document your experiences, challenges, and successes. Reflecting on your journey can help you recognise how far you've come and reinforce your confidence.

Applying Sparring Lessons to Everyday Life

The lessons learned from managing sparring anxiety can extend beyond the dojang and into everyday life. The skills and strategies you develop in Taekwon-Do can help you face various challenges with greater resilience and confidence. Here are some ays to a ply sparring lessons to daily life:

- **STRESS MANAGEMENT**

  The techniques used to manage sparring anxiety, such as breathing exercises, visualisation, and mindfulness, can be applied to everyday stressors. These practices can help you stay calm and focused in high-pressure situations, whether at work, school, or home.

- **RESILIENCE**

  Overcoming sparring anxiety requires perseverance and resilience. The ability to bounce back from setbacks and maintain a positive attitude can be invaluable in everyday life. Developing resilience through sparring can help you navigate life's challenges with greater ease.

- **SELF-CONFIDENCE**

  Building confidence in sparring can translate to increased self-confidence in other areas of life. Believing in your abilities and trusting yourself can empower you to pursue your goals and take on new challenges with determination.

- **EMOTIONAL REGULATION**

  Learning to regulate your emotions during sparring can enhance your emotional intelligence and self-awareness. These skills can improve your relationships, communication, and overall well-being.

- **PROBLEM-SOLVING**

  Sparring involves quick thinking and adaptability. The problem-solving skills you develop in the dojang can help you approach everyday challenges with a strategic and solution-oriented mindset.

THE PATH FORWARD

EMBRACING THE CHALLENGE OF SPARRING

Facing fear is not an easy journey, but it is a profoundly rewarding one. Sparring anxiety, like any form of fear, can be a powerful teacher. It challenges us to confront our limitations, push beyond our comfort zones, and grow as individuals. By understanding the nature of fear and applying practical strategies to manage it, you can transform anxiety into a source of strength and empowerment.

As you continue your journey in Taekwon-Do, remember that fear is a natural part of the process. Embrace it, learn from it, and use it to fuel your growth. The skills and resilience you develop in the dojang will not only enhance your sparring abilities but also enrich your life in countless ways.

In the following chapters, we will explore the intricacies of the fight-or-flight response, delve deeper into the role of adrenaline, and examine practical techniques to tame anxiety. You will learn how sparring can serve as a powerful tool for self-defence and personal development, helping you build a strong mind-body connection and apply these lessons to everyday life.

CHAPTER 02

THE FIGHT OR FLIGHT RESPONSE

UNDERSTANDING YOUR BODY'S REACTIONS

The fight or flight response is a fundamental aspect of human biology and psychology. It is a survival mechanism that has evolved over millions of years, allowing our ancestors to respond quickly to threats. In the context of Taekwon-Do and sparring, understanding this response is crucial for managing fear and anxiety effectively. This chapter delves into the intricacies of the fight or flight response, exploring its physiological basis, psychological impact, and practical implications for martial artists.

THE ORIGINS OF THE FIGHT OR FLIGHT RESPONSE

The fight or flight response, also known as the acute stress response, was first described by physiologist Walter Cannon in the early 20th century. It is an automatic reaction to perceived threats, preparing the body to either confront the danger (fight) or escape from it (flight). This response is deeply embedded in our physiology and is triggered by the sympathetic nervous system.

In the wild, our ancestors faced numerous threats from predators, hostile environments, and other humans. The fight or flight response was essential for survival, enabling quick decision-making and rapid physical reactions. While modern life presents different challenges, the underlying mechanisms of this response remain the same.

THE PHYSIOLOGY OF THE FIGHT OR FLIGHT RESPONSE

When we perceive a threat, the brain's amygdala sends a distress signal to the hypothalamus, which acts as a command centre, communicating with the rest of the body through the autonomic nervous system. This system has two main components: the sympathetic nervous system and the parasympathetic nervous system.

SYMPATHETIC NERVOUS SYSTEM

The sympathetic nervous system triggers the fight or flight response. It signals the adrenal glands to release adrenaline (epinephrine) and norepinephrine into the bloodstream. These hormones cause a series of physiological changes

- **INCREASED HEART RATE AND BLOOD PRESSURE**

   The heart pumps faster to supply muscles with more oxygen and energy.

- **RAPID BREATHING**

   The respiratory rate increases to take in more oxygen.

- **DILATED PUPILS**

   The pupils widen to enhance vision.

- **REDIRECTED BLOOD FLOW**

   Blood is redirected from non-essential functions, like digestion, to the muscles and vital organs.

- **TENSED MUSCLES**

    Muscles become more rigid and ready for action.

- **HEIGHTENED SENSES**

    Vision, hearing, and other senses become more acute.

- **PARASYMPATHETIC NERVOUS SYSTEM**

    After the threat has passed, the parasympathetic nervous system helps to calm the body and restore it to a state of balance (homeostasis). It reduces heart rate, slows breathing, and promotes digestion and relaxation.

PSYCHOLOGICAL IMPACT OF THE FIGHT OR FLIGHT RESPONSE

The fight or flight response not only affects the body but also has significant psychological effects. These mental reactions are crucial for understanding how to manage anxiety and fear in sparring.

- **HEIGHTENED AWARENESS**

    During the fight or flight response, the brain becomes hyper-aware of the environment. This heightened state of alertness can help detect threats quickly but can also lead to hypervigilance and anxiety.

- **NARROWED FOCUS**

    The brain focuses intensely on the perceived threat, which can be beneficial in dangerous situations. However, in sparring, this can sometimes result in tunnel vision, where a practitioner may miss important cues or opportunities.

- **EMOTIONAL INTENSITY**

    The release of adrenaline and other stress hormones can amplify emotions, leading to heightened fear, anger, or aggression. Managing these emotions is critical for maintaining composure in sparring.

- **IMPAIRED COGNITIVE FUNCTION**

    While the fight or flight response can enhance physical performance, it can sometimes impair higher cognitive functions, such as decision-making, problem-solving, and critical thinking. This is because the brain prioritises immediate survival over complex thought processes.

THE FIGHT OR FLIGHT RESPONSE IN SPARRING

Understanding how the fight or flight response manifests in sparring is essential for martial artists. Recognising these reactions can help practitioners develop strategies to manage their anxiety and perform more effectively.

- **IN-THE-MOMENT REACTIONS**

    During sparring, the fight-or-flight response can manifest as physical tension, rapid breathing, and heightened alertness. While these reactions can enhance performance, excessive anxiety can lead to mistakes and impaired judgement. Training to stay calm under pressure is crucial.

- **POST-SPARRING RECOVER**

    After a sparring session, the body needs time to return to a state of balance. Engaging in cool-down exercises, deep breathing, and reflection can help facilitate recovery and prepare for future sessions.

TECHNIQUES FOR MANAGING THE FIGHT OR FLIGHT RESPONSE

Managing the fight or flight response in sparring involves a combination of physical, mental, and emotional strategies. Here are some effective techniques:

- **BREATHING EXERCISES**

    Controlled breathing can help activate the parasympathetic nervous system an dreduce the intensity of the fight or flight response. Techniques such as diaphragmat icbreathing, box breathing, and the 4-7-8 method can calm the mind and body.

- **PROGRESSIVE MUSCLE RELAXATION**

    This technique involves tensing and then relaxing different muscle groups to release physical tension. Practicing progressive muscle relaxation regularly can help reduce overall stress levels.

- **VISUALISATION AND MENTAL REHEARSAL**

    Imagining successful sparring scenarios and rehearsing techniques mentally can build confidence and reduce anxiety. Visualization helps the brain become familiar with sparring situations, making them less intimidating.

- **MINDFULNESS AND MEDITATION**

    Mindfulness practices involve staying present and focused on the current moment without judgement. Meditation can help calm the mind, reduce stress, and improve emotional regulation. Incorporating these practices into daily routines can enhanceoverall well-being and sparring performance.

- **GRADUAL EXPOSURE**

    Gradual exposure to sparring can help desensitise the fight or flight response. Starting with light, controlled sparring and gradually increasing intensity allows the body and mind to adapt to the stressors of sparring.

- **POSITIVE SELF-TALK**

    Replacing negative thoughts with positive affirmations can shift your mindset and reduce anxiety. Developing a set of encouraging statements, such as "I am prepared" or "I can handle this," can build confidence and resilience.

BUILDING RESILIENCE

TURNING STRESS INTO STRENGTH

The fight-or-flight response, while often viewed negatively, can be harnessed to build resilience and strength. By understanding and managing this response, practitioners can turn stress into a powerful tool for personal growth and development.

- **EMBRACE STRESS AS A TEACHER**

    Instead of fearing the fight or flight response, view it as an opportunity to learn and grow. Stress can reveal areas for improvement and highlight strengths that may not have been apparent otherwise.

- **DEVELOP A GROWTH MINDSET**

    Adopting a growth mindset means viewing challenges as opportunities for development rather than obstacles. This perspective can help you stay motivated and resilient in the face of adversity.

- **PRACTISE CONSISTENTLY**

    Regular practice is essential for building resilience. The more you spar and expose yourself to the stressors of martial arts, the more adept you will become at managing the fight-or-flight response.

- **SEEK SUPPORT AND FEEDBACK**

    Surround yourself with supportive peers and instructors who can provide constructive feedback and encouragement. Learning from others and receiving positive reinforcement can boost your confidence and resilience.

APPLYING LESSONS BEYOND THE DOJANG

The skills and strategies developed for managing the fight or flight response in sparring can be applied to various aspects of life. Here are some ways to use these lessons beyond the dojang:

- **STRESS MANAGEMENT**

    The techniques used to calm the fight or flight response, such as breathing exercises and mindfulness, can be applied to everyday stressors. These practices can help you stay calm and focused in high-pressure situations at work, school, or home.

- **EMOTIONAL REGULATION**

    Learning to manage intense emotions during sparring can enhance your emotional intelligence and self-awareness. These skills can improve your relationships, communication, and overall well-being.

- **CONFIDENCE AND RESILIENCE**

    Building confidence and resilience in sparring can translate to other areas of life. Believing in your abilities and staying resilient in the face of challenges can empower you pursue your goals and overcome obstacles.

- **PROBLEM-SOLVING**

    The quick thinking and adaptability required in sparring can enhance your problem-solving skills. Approaching everyday challenges with a strategic and solution-oriented mindset can lead to more effective outcomes.

CONCLUSION

EMBRACING THE FIGHT OR FLIGHT RESPONSE

Understanding the fight or flight response is a crucial step in managing sparring anxiety and improving performance in Taekwon-Do. By recognising the physiological and psychological aspects of this response, practitioners can develop effective strategiesto stay calm, focused, and resilient under pressure.

Embrace the fight or flight response as a natural part of the human experience. Use it as a tool for growth, development, and self-discovery. The lessons learned in managing this response in sparring can enrich your life in countless ways, helping you navigate challenges with confidence and composure.

In the following chapters, we will explore the role of adrenaline in more detail, delve into practical techniques to tame anxiety, and examine how sparring can serve as a powerful tool for self-defence and personal development. Join me as we continue this journey, uncovering the true power of Taekwon-Do and the human spirit.

CHAPTER 03

ADRENALINE

FRIEND OR FOE?

Adrenaline, often referred to as the "fight or flight" hormone, plays a pivotal role in our body's response to stress and danger. For martial artists, particularly those practicing Taekwon-Do, understanding adrenaline's effects is essential for managing fear and optimising performance. This chapter delves into the dual nature of adrenaline, examining how it can be both a powerful ally and a formidable adversary in the sparring ring.

THE SCIENCE OF ADRENALINE

Adrenaline, also known as epinephrine, is a hormone and neurotransmitter produced by the adrenal glands, which sit atop the kidneys. It is released into the bloodstream in response to stress, excitement, or perceived threats, triggering a series of physiological changes designed to enhance the body's ability to cope with immediate danger.

RELEASE AND EFFECTS

When the brain perceives a threat, the hypothalamus signals the adrenal medulla to release adrenaline. This surge of adrenaline prepares the body for rapid action:

- **INCREASED HEART RATE AND BLOOD PRESSURE**

    The heart pumps faster and harder, delivering more oxygen and nutrients to muscles.

- **DILATED AIRWAYS**

    Breathing becomes quicker and deeper, increasing oxygen intake.

- **INCREASED BLOOD SUGAR LEVELS**

    The liver releases glucose, providing a quick energy source for muscles.

- **ENHANCED STRENGTH AND SPEED**

    Muscle efficiency improves, allowing for stronger and faster movements.

- **HEIGHTENED SENSES**

    Vision, hearing, and other senses become more acute, improving situational awareness.

SHORT-TERM AND LONG-TERM EFFECTS

While the short-term effects of adrenaline are beneficial for immediate survival, prolonged exposure can have negative consequences. Chronic stress and frequent adrenaline surges can lead to issues such as high blood pressure, anxiety, and adrenal fatigue.

ADRENALINE AS AN ALLY

Adrenaline can be a powerful ally for martial artists, enhancing physical performance and providing a competitive edge. Here's how adrenaline can be harnessed to improve sparring outcomes:

- **ENHANCED PHYSICAL PERFORMANCE**

    The surge of energy and strength provided by adrenaline can improve speed, power, and endurance. This can be particularly beneficial in high-intensity sparring sessions where quick reactions and powerful techniques are essential.

- **INCREASED FOCUS AND AWARENESS**

    Adrenaline sharpens the senses, heightening awareness of the sparring environment and the opponent's movements. This increased focus can lead to better decision-making and more effective defensive and offensive strategies.

- **BOOSTED CONFIDENCE**

    The adrenaline rush can create a sense of invincibility and confidence. This psychological boost can help overcome fear and hesitation, allowing practitioners to engage more fully in sparring.

- **PAIN TOLERANCE**

    Adrenaline can temporarily reduce the perception of pain, enabling martial artists to continue fighting despite minor injuries or discomfort. This can be advantageous in maintaining performance throughout a sparring match.

ADRENALINE AS A FOE

While adrenaline can enhance performance, it can also become a hindrance if not properly managed. The following are potential pitfalls associated with excessive or poorly controlled adrenaline:

- **OVERSTIMULATION**

    Excessive adrenaline can lead to overstimulation, causing jitteriness, lack of coordination, and decreased precision. This can result in sloppy techniques and increased vulnerability in sparring.

- **IMPAIRED DECISION-MAKING**

    The heightened state of arousal caused by adrenaline can impair cognitive functions, such as decision-making and problem-solving. This can lead to impulsive actions and strategic errors during sparring.

- **TUNNEL VISION**

    Adrenaline can narrow focus excessively, leading to tunnel vision. This can cause practitioners to miss important cues from their environment or opponent, reducing overall situational awareness.

- **EMOTIONAL INSTABILITY**

    The intense emotions triggered by adrenaline, such as fear, anger, or aggression, can be difficult to control. Emotional instability can lead to a loss of composure and an increased likelihood of mistakes in sparring.

- **POST-ADRENALINE CRASH**

    After the adrenaline rush subsides, practitioners may experience fatigue, weakness, and a sense of depletion. This post-adrenaline crash can affect subsequent performance and recovery.

STRATEGIES FOR MANAGING ADRENALINE

Effective management of adrenaline is crucial for optimizing performance and maintaining control during sparring. Here are some strategies to help martial artists harness the benefits of adrenaline while mitigating its potential drawbacks:

- **CONTROLLED BREATHING**

    Deep, controlled breathing can help regulate the body's response to adrenaline, reducing over stimulation and promoting calmness. Techniques such as diaphragmatic breathing and box breathing can be particularly effective.

- **VISUALISATION AND MENTAL REHEARSAL**

    Visualising successful sparring scenarios and mentally rehearsing techniques can prepare the mind and body for the adrenaline surge. This practice can help create a sense of familiarity and control during actual sparring sessions.

- **PROGRESSIVE MUSCLE RELAXATION**

    Progressive muscle relaxation involves tensing and then relaxing different muscle groups to release physical tension. This technique can help manage the physical effects of adrenaline and maintain muscle control.

- **MINDFULNESS AND MEDITATION**

    Mindfulness and meditation practices can enhance emotional regulation and reduce the impact of adrenaline on the mind. These practices promote a state of calmawareness, improving focus and decision-making during sparring.

- **GRADUAL EXPOSURE TO STRESS**

    Gradual exposure to sparring stressors can help desensitise the body and mind to the effects of adrenaline. Starting with light sparring and gradually increasing intensity allows practitioners to build tolerance and control.

- **POSITIVE SELF-TALK**

    Developing a set of positive affirmations can counteract negative thoughts and emotions triggered by adrenaline. Repeating statements such as "I am in control" or "I can handle this" can build confidence and resilience.

PERSONAL REFLECTIONS

ADRENALINE IN MY SPARRING EXPERIENCE

Reflecting on my journey in Taekwon-Do, adrenaline has played a significant role in shaping my sparring experiences. Initially, the adrenaline rush felt overwhelming, amplifying my fears and making it difficult to maintain control. However, through consistent practice and the application of various techniques, I learned to harness adrenaline as a source of strength and focus.

One memorable sparring session stands out in my mind. The anticipation of facing a more experienced opponent triggered a powerful adrenaline surge. My heart raced, my palms sweated, and my mind teetered between excitement and fear. At that moment, I consciously employed controlled breathing and visualisation techniques, imagining myself executing techniques with precision and confidence. This will be covered in my next book on targeting and with precision.

As the match began, I felt the adrenaline coursing through my veins. Instead of succumbing to the intensity, I channelled the energy into my movements. My strikes were faster, my blocks more precise, and my awareness heightened. The adrenaline became an ally, propelling me to perform at my best.

After the match, I experienced the familiar post-adrenaline crash, feeling a wave of exhaustion. However, the sense of accomplishment and the knowledge that I had successfully managed the adrenaline surge left me with a profound sense of empowerment.

ADRENALINE IN EVERYDAY LIFE

The lessons learned from managing adrenaline in sparring can be applied to various aspects of life. Here are some ways to harness adrenaline effectively beyond the dojang:

- **PUBLIC SPEAKING**

    Adrenaline is a common response to public speaking. By applying controlled breathing, visualisation, and positive self-talk, you can transform nervous energy into dynamic and engaging presentations.

- **HIGH-PRESSURE SITUATIONS**

    In high-pressure situations, such as job interviews or important meetings, the ability to manage adrenaline can enhance performance. Techniques like mindfulness and progressive muscle relaxation can help you stay calm and focused.

- **PHYSICAL CHALLENGES**

    Adrenaline can be a powerful ally in physical challenges, such as athletic competitions or demanding workouts. Learning to channel adrenaline effectively can improve endurance, strength, and overall performance.

- **STRESSFUL EVENTS**

    Life is full of stressful events, from exams to personal conflicts. By understanding and managing the body's response to adrenaline, you can navigate these challenges with greater resilience and composure.

CONCLUSION

EMBRACING ADRENALINE

Adrenaline is a complex and powerful force that can significantly impact performance in sparring and beyond. By understanding its dual nature and learning to manage its effects, martial artists can harness adrenaline as a valuable ally while mitigating its potential drawbacks.

Embrace adrenaline as a natural part of the human experience. Use it to fuel your growth, enhance your performance, and build resilience. The skills and strategies developed in managing adrenaline in sparring can enrich your life, helping you face challenges with confidence and composure.

In the following chapters, we will explore practical techniques to tame anxiety, delve into the role of mental conditioning in sparring, and examine how the lessons learned in Taekwon-Do can be applied to everyday life. Join me as we continue this journey, uncovering the true power of adrenaline and the human spirit.

CHAPTER 04

THE MIND-BODY CONNECTION

HARNESSING MENTAL STRENGTH

The journey of mastering Taekwon-Do is not just about physical prowess; it's equally about mental resilience. The mind-body connection plays a crucial role in how effectively we can perform, especially under the pressure of sparring. In this chapter, I will share my struggles and how understanding and harnessing mental strength transformed my approach to Taekwon-Do and life itself.

UNDERSTANDING THE MIND-BODY CONNECTION

The mind-body connection refers to the relationship between our mental state and physical performance. Our thoughts, emotions, and attitudes can significantly impact our physical abilities, and vice versa. This connection is particularly evident in martial arts, where mental clarity, focus, and confidence can enhance physical execution and endurance.

- **PSYCHOSOMATIC RESPONSES**

    Our body responds to mental states through psychosomatic responses. Stress and anxiety can manifest as physical symptoms like increased heart rate, muscle tension, and reduced coordination. Conversely, a calm and focused mind can enhance physical performance by promoting relaxation, precision, and fluidity in movements.

- **NEUROPLASTICITY**

    The brain's ability to reorganise itself by forming new neural connections is known as neuroplasticity. This means that through consistent practice and mental conditioning, we can train our mind to respond more effectively to stress and improve our physical skills.

- **EMOTIONAL REGULATION**

    Managing emotions is crucial in maintaining the mind-body connection. Techniques like mindfulness and emotional regulation help in staying calm and composed, which directly influences physical performance.

MY STRUGGLES WITH MENTAL STRENGTH

My journey in Taekwon-Do has been deeply intertwined with my personal struggles, particularly my battle with severe social anxiety. Stepping into the dojang for the first time was daunting. The fear of judgement, failure, and physical confrontation loomed large, often paralyzing me with anxiety.

- **INITIAL CHALLENGES**

    In the beginning, my anxiety manifested physically. My hands would shake, my heart would race, and my movements would become erratic. The disconnect between my mind and body was glaringly apparent, making it difficult to execute techniques with precision.

- **FEAR OF SPARRING**

    Sparring sessions were the most challenging. The prospect of facing an opponent triggered intense fear and self-doubt. My mind would be consumed with negative thoughts, questioning my abilities and anticipating failure. This mental turmoil would translate into stiff and uncoordinated movements, making me an easy target.

- **PERSONAL LIFE IMPACT**

    Outside the dojang, my struggles with mental strength affected my personal and professional life. The stress from the business I was running, coupled with my homelessness, exacerbated my anxiety. The inability to manage my mental state hindered my ability to perform both in Taekwon-Do and in daily life.

TECHNIQUES TO HARNESS MENTAL STRENGTH

Through my journey, I discovered several techniques that helped me harness mental strength and bridge the mind-body connection. These techniques have been instrumental in transforming my approach to Taekwon-Do and managing my anxiety.

- **MINDFULNESS AND MEDITATION**

    Practicing mindfulness and meditation has been a cornerstone in my mental conditioning. By focusing on the present moment and observing my thoughts without judgement, I learned to reduce the grip of anxiety. Meditation helped me cultivate a sense of inner calm and clarity, which translated into more controlled and precise movements in sparring.

- **VISUALISATION**

    Visualisation involves mentally rehearsing techniques and sparring scenarios. Before each session, I would close my eyes and visualize myself executing techniques flawlessly and responding to my opponent with confidence. This mental rehearsal created a sense of familiarity and prepared my mind for the physical challenges.

- **BREATHING TECHNIQUES**

    Controlled breathing techniques, such as diaphragmatic breathing and box breathing, helped regulate my physiological responses to stress. Deep, slow breaths would calm my racing heart and relax my tense muscles, allowing me to maintain composure during sparring.

- **POSITIVE SELF-TALK**

    Replacing negative thoughts with positive affirmations was crucial in building mental strength. I developed a set of affirmations, such as "I am capable," "I am in control," and "I can handle this." Repeating these statements helped counteract self-doubt and instil a sense of confidence.

- **PROGRESSIVE MUSCLE RELAXATION**

    This technique involves tensing and then relaxing different muscle groups. It helped me become more aware of physical tension and provided a method to release it. This practice was particularly useful before and after sparring sessions to maintain physical relaxation and mental focus.

OVERCOMING PERSONAL STRUGGLES

As I applied these techniques consistently, I began to notice a significant shift in my performance and overall well-being.

- **IMPROVED SPARRING PERFORMANCE**

    My sparring sessions became more effective as I learned to manage my anxiety. With a calm mind, my movements became more fluid and coordinated. I could anticipate my opponent's actions better and respond with greater precision and confidence.

- **ENHANCED MENTAL RESILIENCE**

    Beyond Taekwon-Do, these mental conditioning techniques helped me build resilience in the face of life's challenges. I became better equipped to handle stress, whether it was related to my business, personal life, or financial struggles.

- **PERSONAL GROWTH**

    Embracing the mind-body connection facilitated significant personal growth. I gained a deeper understanding of myself and my capabilities. The journey of overcoming my mental struggles through Taekwon-Do became a source of empowerment, shaping my identity and strengthening my resolve.

- **HOLISTIC WELL-BEING**

    The integration of mental and physical practices promoted holistic well-being. My overall health improved as I learned to manage stress and anxiety more effectively. This balance positively impacted my relationships, work, and daily life.

THE BROADER IMPACT OF MENTAL STRENGTH

The principles of the mind-body connection and mental strength extend beyond martial arts. Here are some broader applications of these techniques:

- **PROFESSIONAL SUCCESS**

    Mental conditioning techniques can enhance performance in professional settings. Visualization, positive self-talk, and mindfulness can improve focus, creativity, and problem-solving abilities.

- **STRESS MANAGEMENT**

    Understanding and managing the mind-body connection is crucial in stress management. Techniques like controlled breathing and progressive muscle relaxation can help you navigate stressful situations with composure.

- **PERSONAL DEVELOPMENT**

    Building mental strength fosters personal development. It encourages self-awareness, emotional regulation, and resilience, which are essential for personal growth and fulfillment.

CONCLUSION

EMBRACING MENTAL STRENGTH

Harnessing mental strength through the mind-body connection has been a transformative journey. My struggles with anxiety and the challenges I faced in Taekwon-Do revealed the profound impact of mental resilience on physical performance and overall well-being. By integrating mindfulness, visualisation, controlled breathing, and positive self-talk into my practice, I bridged the gap between mind and body, unlocking new levels of performance and personal growth.

The lessons learned from this journey extend far beyond the dojang. Embracing the mind-body connection equips us with the tools to navigate life's challenges with confidence and composure. Whether in martial arts, professional endeavours, or personal pursuits, the power of mental strength can propel us toward success and fulfilment.

In the next chapters, we will explore practical techniques to tame anxiety, delve deeper into the role of mental conditioning in sparring, and examine how the principles of Taekwon-Do can be applied to everyday life. Join me as we continue this journey, uncovering the true potential of the mind-body connection and the human spirit.

CHAPTER 05

BUILDING CONFIDENCE

THE FIRST STEPS IN TAEKWON-DO

Starting Taekwon-Do can be an intimidating experience, especially for those of us who struggle with anxiety and self-doubt. The moment you step into the dojang, you're not just competing against others; you're also competing against your own insecurities and fears. However, it's in this very environment that you have the opportunity to grow, build confidence, and discover your true potential. In this chapter, I'll share my personal journey of taking those first steps in Taekwon-Do.

THE DAUNTING FIRST STEP

Walking into the dojang for the first time was a monumental challenge for me. My severe social anxiety made it difficult to be around people, let alone participate in a group activity. The fear of judgement and failure was overwhelming, and I constantly questioned whether I belonged in such a disciplined and demanding environment.

- **INITIAL ANXIETY**

    The first few classes were filled with trepidation. The unfamiliar surroundings, the structured routines, and the presence of experienced practitioners all contributed to a sense of being out of place. My heart would race, my palms would sweat, and my mind would be clouded with self-doubt.

- **PERCEIVED COMPETITION**

    It felt as though everyone was watching and judging my every move. I was not just competing with others but also with the critical voice in my head that kept telling me I wasn't good enough. The pressure to perform and keep up with the class added to the anxiety.

- **STARTING SLOW**

    I quickly realized that to overcome these feelings, I needed to shift my focus. Instead of comparing myself to others, I began to concentrate on my own progress. Starting slow and setting realistic goals became my strategy. I decided to focus on the level I was at, rather than where I thought I should be.

THE GROWTH MINDSET

Adopting a growth mindset was crucial in building my confidence. This mindset emphasized that abilities and skills could be developed through dedication and hard work. It shifted my perspective from fear of failure to embracing challenges as opportunities for growth.v

- **SMALL VICTORIES**

    Celebrating small victories was essential. Whether it was mastering a basic technique or simply showing up to class consistently, each achievement, no matter how minor, became a stepping stone towards building confidence.

- **POSITIVE REINFORCEMENT**

    Positive reinforcement from instructors and fellow students played a significant role. Their encouragement and constructive feedback helped me see my potential and motivated me to keep pushing forward.

- **PERSONAL PROGRESS**

    Keeping track of personal progress helped me stay motivated. I maintained a journal where I noted down improvements, challenges, and reflections after each class. This practice not only highlighted my growth but also served as a reminder of my commitment and resilience.

THE ROLE OF INSTRUCTORS AND PEERS

The support from instructors and peers was instrumental in my journey. Their guidance, encouragement, and camaraderie created a nurturing environment where I could grow and build confidence.

- **INSTRUCTOR SUPPORT**

    My instructors were patient and understanding, recognizing my struggles and offering tailored guidance. Their belief in my abilities, even when I doubted myself, was a powerful motivator. They emphasized progress over perfection and encouraged me to focus on the process rather than the outcome.

- **PEER ENCOURAGEMENT**

    The sense of community within the dojang was a source of strength. Fellow students, regardless of their skill level, offered support and camaraderie. Sharing experiences, challenges, and victories with peers created a bond that made the journey less daunting and more enjoyable.

- **MENTORSHIP**

    Finding a mentor within the dojang can be incredibly beneficial. My mentor provided personalized advice, shared their own experiences, and helped me navigate the challenges of Taekwon-Do. Their guidance was invaluable in building my confidence and skills.

PERSONAL REFLECTIONS

MY JOURNEY OF BUILDING CONFIDENCE

Reflecting on my journey, there were several key moments and lessons that significantly contributed to building my confidence in Taekwon-Do and beyond.

- **FACING FEAR HEAD-ON**

    One of the most transformative experiences was participating in my first sparring session. The fear of physical confrontation was intense, but facing it head-on taught me that I was stronger and more capable than I had imagined. Each sparring session became an opportunity to push my limits and grow.

- **EMBRACING MISTAKES**

    Learning to embrace mistakes as part of the learning process was a significant shift. Instead of seeing mistakes as failures, I began to view them as valuable feedback. This change in perspective reduced my fear of failure and allowed me to take risks and experiment with new techniques.

- **PHYSICAL AND MENTAL TRANSFORMATION**

    As my skills improved, so did my physical fitness and mental resilience. The physical demands of Taekwon-Do required discipline and perseverance, which translated into increased confidence in my abilities. The mental conditioning, such as mindfulness and visualization, strengthened my focus and composure.

- **APPLICATION IN DAILY LIFE**

    The confidence I built in Taekwon-Do extended to other areas of my life. Whether it was handling stress at work, navigating personal challenges, or pursuing new opportunities, the lessons learned in the dojang equipped me with the confidence to face life's uncertainties with courage and determination.

PRACTICAL TIPS FOR BUILDING CONFIDENCE

Based on my experiences, here are some practical tips for building confidence in Taekwon-Do:

- **SET REALISTIC GOALS**

    Start with small, achievable goals and gradually increase the difficulty. This approach helps build a sense of accomplishment and motivation.

- **FOCUS ON PERSONAL PROGRESS**

    Concentrate on your own progress rather than comparing yourself to others. Celebrate your achievements, no matter how small.

- **SEEK FEEDBACK**

    Constructive feedback from instructors and peers is invaluable. Use it to identify areas for improvement and track your progress.

- **PRACTISE CONSISTENTLY**

    Consistency is key to building skills and confidence. Regular practice reinforces techniques and builds muscle memory.

- **EMBRACE CHALLENGES**

    View challenges as opportunities for growth. Step out of your comfort zone and push your limits.

- **STAY POSITIVE**

    Cultivate a positive mindset. Use positive affirmations and visualise success to boost confidence.

- **FIND A MENTOR**
  Seek a mentor who can provide guidance, support, and personalised advice.

CONCLUSION

THE PATH TO CONFIDENCE

Building confidence in Taekwon-Do is a journey that extends beyond the physical realm. It involves mental resilience, a growth mindset, and a supportive community. My personal struggles with anxiety and self-doubt were significant barriers, but through Taekwon-Do, I found the tools and support to overcome them.

Starting slow, focusing on personal progress, and embracing challenges were key strategies in my journey. The lessons learned in the dojang have not only transformed my approach to martial arts but also enriched my life, helping me navigate challenges with confidence and determination.

In the following chapters, we will delve deeper into techniques for taming anxiety, the role of mental conditioning in sparring, and how the principles of Taekwon-Do can be applied to everyday life. Join me as we continue this journey, uncovering the true potential of confidence and the human spirit.

CHAPTER 06

TECHNIQUES TO TAME ANXIETY

PRACTICAL EXERCISES

Anxiety, particularly in the context of Taekwon-Do sparring, can be a formidable barrier to progress. It's a challenge I faced personally, often feeling overwhelmed by the prospect of physical confrontation and the pressure to perform. Over time, I discovered several practical exercises that helped tame my anxiety and allowed me to approach sparring with greater confidence. This chapter delves into these techniques and how they can be applied to manage anxiety, both in the dojang and beyond.

ACCEPTING THE WORST-CASE SCENARIO

One of the most liberating realisations in my journey was accepting the worst-case scenario. By confronting my deepest fears and understanding that they were often exaggerated, I was able to reduce their power over me.

- **WORST-CASE SCENARIO EXERCISE**

  Sit down and write out your worst fears related to sparring. What's the absolute worst that could happen? Maybe you imagine getting hurt, losing badly, or embarrassing yourself. Once these fears are articulated, challenge them. Ask yourself how likely they are and what steps you can take to mitigate them. This exercise helps in rationalising fears and making them more manageable.

- **PULLING BACK FROM FEAR**

  Once you've identified the worst-case scenario, work backward. What are the realistic outcomes, and how can you prepare for them? This approach helps in shifting the focus from fear to proactive problem-solving.

PHYSICAL PREPARATION

MANAGING ENERGY LEVELS

Managing physical energy is crucial in handling anxiety. For me, the fear of Taekwon-Do often meant I had too much nervous energy. I found that tiring myself out before class helped me manage this excess energy, making anxiety easier to handle.

- **PRE-CLASS WORKOUTS**

  Engaging in a rigorous workout before class, such as running or lifting weights, can help expand nervous energy. This approach leaves you physically tired, which can reduce the intensity of anxiety symptoms. However, it's important to balance this so you're not too exhausted to participate effectively in class.

- **ENERGY MANAGEMENT**

  Over time, I learned to manage my energy more effectively. Instead of completely exhausting myself, I found a balance where I was active enough to reduce anxiety but still had enough energy for sparring.

MINDFULNESS AND BREATHING TECHNIQUES

Mindfulness and controlled breathing have been powerful tools in my anxiety management toolkit. These techniques help calm the mind and body, making it easier to focus and perform during sparring.

- **MINDFULNESS MEDITATION**

Practicing mindfulness meditation involves focusing on the present moment without judgement. Before sparring, spend a few minutes in a quiet space, focusing on your breath and letting go of anxious thoughts. This practice helps in centering your mind and reducing anxiety.

- **CONTROLLED BREATHING**

Techniques such as diaphragmatic breathing or box breathing can help regulate your physiological response to anxiety. Deep, slow breaths signal to your body that it's safe to relax. Use these techniques before and during sparring to maintain calm and focus.

VISUALISATION AND POSITIVE SELF-TALK

Visualisation and positive self-talk are mental techniques that prepare your mind for the challenges of sparring. They help build confidence and reduce the impact of negative thoughts.

- **VISUALISATION**

    Spend time visualising successful sparring sessions. Imagine yourself executing techniques flawlessly, responding to your opponent with confidence, and handling any challenges that arise. This mental rehearsal creates a sense of familiarity and boosts confidence.

- **POSITIVE SELF-TALK**

    Replace negative thoughts with positive affirmations. Create a set of affirmations that resonate with you, such as "I am capable," "I am strong," and "I can handle this." Repeat these affirmations before and during sparring to reinforce a positive mindset.

PRACTICAL SPARRING TECHNIQUES

When it comes to actual sparring, several practical techniques can help manage anxiety and improve performance.

- **START SLOW**

    Begin with light sparring sessions where the focus is on technique rather than intensity. Gradually increase the level of contact and complexity as you become more comfortable. This gradual exposure helps build confidence and reduces anxiety.

- **CONTROLLED ENVIRONMENT**

    Practice sparring in a controlled environment where you feel safe and supported. Communicate with your partner about your anxiety and agree on a pace that suits both of you. This mutual understanding creates a more relaxed atmosphere.

- **FOCUS ON BASICS**

  Concentrate on mastering basic techniques before attempting advanced moves. Building a strong foundation instils confidence and makes it easier to handle the demands of sparring.

- **SET ACHIEVABLE GOALS**

  Set small, achievable goals for each sparring session. Whether it's landing a specific technique or maintaining your composure, these goals provide a sense of accomplishment and motivation.

- **DEBRIEFING**

  After each sparring session, take time to reflect on what went well and what could be improved. Discuss these points with your instructor or partner to gain insights and develop strategies for future sessions.

PERSONAL REFLECTIONS

MY JOURNEY WITH SPARRING ANXIETY

My personal journey with sparring anxiety has been filled with ups and downs. Accepting the worst-case scenario was a turning point, as it allowed me to confront my fears directly. Managing my physical energy through pre-class workouts helped me approach sparring sessions with a calmer mindset.

- **FACING THE FEAR OF SPARRING**

  Initially, sparring was my biggest fear in Taekwon-Do. The thought of facing an opponent triggered intense anxiety. However, by using the techniques mentioned above, I gradually became more comfortable. Each sparring session was a step toward overcoming my fears.

- **PHYSICAL EXHAUSTION VS. ANXIETY**

  There were times when I would tire myself out to the point of exhaustion before class, thinking it would make anxiety more manageable. While it worked to some extent, I realized that balance was key. Finding the right level of physical activity helped reduce anxiety without depleting my energy.

- **MENTAL CONDITIONING**

  Visualisation and positive self-talk became integral parts of my preparation. Before each session, I would visualize success and repeat affirmations to build confidence. This mental conditioning helped me stay focused and perform better during sparring.

- **SUPPORTIVE ENVIRONMENT**

  The support from my instructors and peers was invaluable. Their understanding and encouragement created a safe space where I could face my fears and grow. Discussing my anxiety openly helped me feel less isolated and more supported.

- **PROGRESS OVER PERFECTION**

    Focusing on progress rather than perfection was a crucial lesson. Each small improvement, whether in technique or mental resilience, was a victory. This mindset shift reduced the pressure I placed on myself and made the journey more enjoyable.

CONCLUSION

EMBRACING THE JOURNEY

Taming anxiety, especially in the context of Taekwon-Do sparring, is a continuous journey. It requires a combination of mental and physical techniques, a supportive environment, and a willingness to face fears head-on. My personal experiences have taught me that while anxiety can be a formidable opponent, it is possible to manage and even overcome it.

By accepting the worst-case scenario, managing physical energy, practicing mindfulness and breathing techniques, and using visualization and positive self-talk, I have been able to build confidence and improve my sparring performance. These techniques have not only enhanced my Taekwon-Do journey but also provided valuable tools for managing anxiety in daily life.

As we move forward, the next chapters will explore more advanced strategies for mental conditioning, the importance of resilience, and how the principles of Taekwon-Do can be applied to broader aspects of life. Join me as we continue this journey, uncovering the true potential of the human spirit in the face of anxiety and fear

CHAPTER 07

SPARRING AS SELF-DEFENSE

REAL-WORLD APPLICATIONS

Taekwon-Do sparring is not only a valuable aspect of martial arts training but also an essential skill for self-defence in real-world situations. Understanding why we experience adrenaline dumps and how to manage them is crucial for effective self-defence. In this chapter, we'll explore the physiological responses to sparring and competition, the psychological aspects of handling pressure, and how to apply sparring techniques in real-world self-defence scenarios.

THE ADRENALINE DUMP

UNDERSTANDING THE RUSH

When faced with a threatening situation, our bodies undergo a series of physiological changes known as the "fight or flight" response. This response is triggered by the release of adrenaline, a hormone that prepares the body to either confront the threat or escape from it.

- **THE SCIENCE OF ADRENALINE**

    Adrenaline is produced by the adrenal glands and is released into the bloodstream during moments of stress or danger. It increases heart rate, blood flow to muscles, and energy levels, preparing the body for rapid action.

- **ADRENALINE IN SPARRING**

    Even in a controlled environment like a Taekwon-Do class, sparring can trigger small secretions of adrenaline. The anticipation of physical contact, the need to react quickly, and the competitive aspect of sparring all contribute to this physiological response.

- **ADRENALINE IN COMPETITION**

    The intensity of competition amplifies the adrenaline response. The pressure to perform well, the presence of spectators, and the unfamiliarity of opponents can cause a significant adrenaline dump. This can lead to symptoms such as increased heart rate, rapid breathing, sweaty palms, and a heightened sense of alertness.

PSYCHOLOGICAL ASPECTS OF HANDLING PRESSURE

The psychological impact of sparring and competition can be as challenging as the physical demands. Managing pressure and maintaining composure are critical skills for effective performance.

- **MENTAL PREPARATION**

    Mental conditioning is essential for handling the stress of sparring and competition. Techniques such as visualisation, positive self-talk, and mindfulness help prepare the mind to stay calm and focused.

- **EMOTIONAL REGULATION**

    Learning to regulate emotions during high-pressure situations is crucial. Techniques such as controlled breathing, mindfulness meditation, and grounding exercises can help manage anxiety and prevent it from overwhelming you.

- **EXPERIENCE AND EXPOSURE**

    Regular exposure to sparring and competition helps desensitise the body and mind to the stress response. The more you practise under pressure, the more adept you become at managing adrenaline and maintaining performance.

REAL-WORLD APPLICATIONS

SELF-DEFENSE

Applying sparring techniques in real-world self-defence scenarios requires a deep understanding of both the physical and psychological aspects of combat. Here's how to focus on making sparring skills effective in real-life situations.

- **AWARENESS AND AVOIDANCE**

    The first step in self-defence is awareness. Being mindful of your surroundings and potential threats can help you avoid dangerous situations. In sparring, this translates to maintaining focus and awareness of your opponent's movements and intentions.

- **CONTROLLED RESPONSE**

    In a real-world confrontation, managing your adrenaline response is crucial. Techniques learned in sparring, such as controlled breathing and staying calm under pressure, can help you maintain composure and think clearly.

- **EFFECTIVE TECHNIQUES**

    Focus on mastering fundamental techniques that are practical and effective in realworld situations. This includes strikes, blocks, and evasive manoeuvers that can be executed quickly and efficiently under stress.

- **ADAPTABILITY**

    Real-world self-defence requires adaptability. Unlike sparring, where rules and predictability exist, street encounters can be chaotic and unpredictable. Train to react to various scenarios and adapt your techniques as needed.

- **DECISION-MAKING**

    Effective self-defene involves quick and decisive actions. In sparring, practice making rapid decisions about when to attack, defend, or retreat. This decision-making ability is critical in real-world situations where hesitation can be dangerous.

PERSONAL REFLECTIONS

MY EXPERIENCE WITH ADRENALINE AND SELF-DEFENSE

Throughout my Taekwon-Do journey, managing adrenaline and applying sparring skills in real-world contexts have been significant challenges. Here are some personal reflections on these experiences.

- **ADRENALINE MANAGEMENT**

    I vividly recall the first time I experienced an adrenaline dump during a competition. The intensity of the moment was overwhelming, and my heart felt like it was going to burst out of my chest. Over time, I learned to manage this response through mental conditioning and controlled breathing. Each competition became an opportunity to refine these skills.

- **REAL-WORLD ENCOUNTER**

    There was a moment when I had to apply my sparring skills in a real-world situation. The fear and adrenaline were immense, but the training kicked in. The awareness, controlled response, and effective techniques I had practiced helped me navigate the situation safely. This experience reinforced the importance of regular, realistic training.

- **PRESSURE HANDLING**

    The psychological pressure of sparring and competition taught me valuable lessons about handling stress. The ability to stay calm, make quick decisions, and execute techniques effectively under pressure has been beneficial beyond the dojang, helping me manage stress in various aspects of life.

PRACTICAL EXERCISES FOR REAL-WORLD APPLICATIONS

To effectively apply sparring skills in self-defene, incorporate these practical exercises into your training routine:

- **SCENARIO TRAINING**

    Practice sparring scenarios that mimic real-world situations. This can include defending against multiple opponents, handling surprise attacks, and reacting to various threat levels.

- **STRESS DRILLS**

    Engage in drills that elevate your heart rate and simulate the stress of a real encounter. This can involve high-intensity interval training (HIIT) followed by sparring or selfdefense techniques to replicate the adrenaline dump.

- **SITUATIONAL AWARENESS**

    Incorporate situational awareness exercises into your training. Practisc identifying potential threats, maintaining awareness of your surroundings, and reacting appropriately.

- **DECISION-MAKING DRILLS**

    Create drills that require quick decision-making. For example, have a partner randomly attack with different techniques, and practice deciding whether to block, evade, or counterattack.

- **EMOTIONAL REGULATION TECHNIQUES**

    Regularly practice mindfulness, controlled breathing, and other emotional regulation techniques. These exercises help maintain composure and clear thinking in high-pressure situations.

CONCLUSION

MASTERING SPARRING FOR SELF-DEFENSE

Sparring in Taekwon-Do is not just about competing in the dojang; it's a critical component of self-defense training. Understanding and managing the adrenaline response, handling psychological pressure, and applying effective techniques are essential skills for real-world encounters.

Through personal experience, I have learned that mastering these aspects requires a combination of mental and physical conditioning, practical training, and continuous exposure to challenging situations. By integrating these elements into your Taekwon-Do practice, you can enhance your ability to defend yourself effectively and confidently.

As we continue this journey, the next chapters will delve into more advanced strategies for integrating mental and physical training, the importance of resilience, and how the principles of Taekwon-Do can be applied to various aspects of life. Join me as we explore the true potential of martial arts as a tool for personal growth, self-defense, and overcoming life's challenges.

CHAPTER 08

FROM THE DOJANG TO DAILY LIFE

APPLYING LESSONS BEYOND SPARRING

Taekwon-Do, with its rich philosophy and rigorous training, offers lessons that extend far beyond the dojang. The discipline, focus, and resilience developed through sparring and other practices can be applied to various aspects of daily life. In this chapter, we will explore how the principles and skills learned in Taekwon-Do can enhance personal growth, manage stress, and improve overall well-being.

DISCIPLINE

BUILDING A STRONG FOUNDATION

Discipline is a cornerstone of Taekwon-Do and is crucial for success in both martial arts and everyday life. The structured routines and consistent practice instill a sense of responsibility and commitment.

- **ESTABLISHING ROUTINE**

    Taekwon-Do training emphasizes the importance of regular practice and adhering to a schedule. This discipline can be translated into daily life by establishing consistent routines for work, exercise, and personal development.

- **GOAL SETTING**

    Setting and achieving goals in Taekwon-Do, such as mastering a new technique or earning a higher belt, teaches the value of perseverance and long-term planning. Apply this approach to personal and professional goals by breaking them down into manageable steps and celebrating small victories along the way.

- **TIME MANAGEMENT**

    The need to balance training with other responsibilities teaches effective time management. Prioritizing tasks and creating a balanced schedule can lead to a more productive and fulfilling daily life.

DISCIPLINE

CULTIVATING MINDFULNESS AND CONCENTRATION

The ability to maintain focus during sparring and training is a valuable skill that can be applied to many areas of life.

- **MINDFULNESS PRACTICE**

  The concentration required for executing precise techniques and staying aware of an opponent's movements enhances mindfulness. Incorporate mindfulness practices, such as meditation or focused breathing, into daily routines to improve concentration and reduce stress.

- **ATTENTION TO DETAIL**

  The meticulous attention to form and technique in Taekwon-Do encourages a similar approach to tasks outside the dojang. Whether it's work-related projects or personal hobbies, paying close attention to detail leads to higher quality results and a deeper sense of satisfaction.`

- **PRESENT MOMENT AWARENESS**

  Sparring demands that practitioners stay fully present, responding to immediate challenges without distraction. Apply this principle to everyday activities by engaging fully in the present moment, improving both performance and enjoyment.

RESILIENCE

OVERCOMING CHALLENGES

Resilience is built through the physical and mental challenges encountered in Taekwon-Do. This resilience can be a powerful tool for navigating life's obstacles.

- **FACING ADVERSITY**

  The experience of facing and overcoming challenges in Taekwon-Do, such as difficult sparring sessions or tough training regimens, builds mental toughness. Use this resilience to tackle challenges in daily life, viewing them as opportunities for growth rather than setbacks.

- **STRESS MANAGEMENT**

  The ability to stay calm and focused under pressure, developed through sparring, is invaluable for managing stress in everyday situations. Techniques such as controlled breathing and positive self-talk, practiced during training, can be used to navigate stressful events effectively.

- **ADAPTABILITY**

  Sparring requires quick thinking and adaptability to changing circumstances. This skill is equally important in daily life, where flexibility and the ability to adjust to unexpected changes can lead to better problem-solving and reduced anxiety.

CONFIDENCE

EMPOWERING PERSONAL GROWTH

The confidence gained through Taekwon-Do can enhance various aspects of life, from personal interactions to professional endeavors.

- **SELF-ESTEEM**

    Achieving milestones in Taekwon-Do, such as learning new techniques or progressing through belt ranks, boosts self-esteem. This increased confidence can improve self-image and encourage the pursuit of new challenges in other areas of life.

- **PUBLIC SPEAKING**

    The confidence developed in the dojang can translate into improved public speaking skills. The ability to stay calm and composed while performing in front of others can make presenting ideas or speaking in meetings less intimidating.

- **ASSERTIVENESS**

    Sparring teaches assertiveness and the ability to stand one's ground. This assertiveness can be applied to personal and professional interactions.

PERSONAL REFLECTIONS

APPLYING TAEKWON-DO LESSONS

My journey in Taekwon-Do has profoundly influenced my approach to daily life. Here are some personal reflections on how the lessons learned in the dojang have enriched my life outside of martial arts.

- **ROUTINE AND STRUCTURE**

    The discipline of regular Taekwon-Do practice helped me establish a structured daily routine. This consistency has improved my productivity and provided a sense of stability, especially during challenging times.

- **MINDFULNESS AND FOCUS**

    The focus required in sparring has enhanced my ability to concentrate on tasks and be present in the moment. This mindfulness has improved my work efficiency and deepened my enjoyment of personal activities.

- **RESILIENCE IN ADVERSITY**

    The resilience developed through Taekwon-Do training has been invaluable in facing life's challenges. From managing work-related stress to personal setbacks, the mental toughness gained in the dojang has helped me navigate these obstacles with greater ease.

- **INCREASED CONFIDENCE**

    The confidence gained from progressing in Taekwon-Do has empowered me to take on new challenges and pursue personal goals with greater determination. This self-assurance has positively impacted my professional growth and personal relationships.

PRACTICAL APPLICATIONS FOR DAILY LIFE

To apply the lessons from Taekwon-Do in daily life, consider incorporating the following practices:

- **SET CLEAR GOALS**

    Define personal and professional goals and create a plan to achieve them. Use the discipline and goal-setting techniques learned in Taekwon-Do to stay committed and motivated.

- **PRACTICE MINDFULNESS**

    Incorporate mindfulness practices into your daily routine. This can include meditation, focused breathing exercises, or simply taking a few moments to center yourself before starting a task.

- **BUILD RESILIENCE**

    Embrace challenges as opportunities for growth. Reflect on past experiences in Taekwon-Do where you overcame obstacles and apply the same resilience to current challenges.

- **ENHANCE FOCUS**

    Practice staying present and focused on the task at hand. Minimize distractions and engage fully in each activity, whether it's work-related or a personal hobby.

- **BOOST CONFIDENCE**

    Celebrate your achievements and recognize your progress, both in Taekwon-Do and other areas of life. Use this confidence to pursue new challenges and advocate for yourself.

CONCLUSION

EMBRACING THE TAEKWON-DO PHILOSOPHY

The principles and skills developed through Taekwon-Do extend far beyond the dojang, offering valuable tools for personal growth and improved well-being. By applying the lessons of discipline, focus, resilience, and confidence to daily life, you can navigate challenges more effectively and achieve a greater sense of fulfillment.

As we continue this journey, the next chapters will delve into advanced strategies for integrating mental and physical training, the importance of resilience, and how the principles of Taekwon-Do can be applied to various aspects of life. Join me as we explore the true potential of martial arts as a tool for personal growth, self-defense, and overcoming life's challenges.

CHAPTER 09

OVERCOMING SOCIAL ANXIETY

A PERSONAL JOURNEY IN TAEKWON-DO

Social anxiety can be a debilitating condition, making even the simplest social interactions feel overwhelming. For many, the fear of judgment, rejection, or embarrassment can hinder personal growth and limit opportunities. My journey in Taekwon-Do has been instrumental in helping me confront and manage my social anxiety. In this chapter, I will share how Taekwon-Do has provided a supportive environment for overcoming social fears and building confidence.

UNDERSTANDING SOCIAL ANXIETY

Before delving into my personal experiences, it's important to understand what social anxiety entails and how it can impact various aspects of life.

- **DEFINITION AND SYMPTOMS**

    Social anxiety is characterized by an intense fear of social situations where one may be scrutinized by others. Common symptoms include excessive self-consciousness, fear of embarrassment, avoidance of social interactions, and physical symptoms such as sweating, trembling, and rapid heartbeat.

- **IMPACT ON LIFE**

    Social anxiety can significantly impact personal and professional life. It may lead to avoidance of social gatherings, difficulties in forming relationships, and challenges in work environments where interaction is required.

MY JOURNEY WITH SOCIAL ANXIETY

My battle with social anxiety began early in life. The fear of being judged or rejected made social interactions extremely challenging. However, discovering Taekwon-Do opened up new possibilities for managing and eventually overcoming these fears.

- **JOINING TAEKWON-DO**

    Taking the first step to join a Taekwon-Do class was daunting. Walking into a room full of strangers, each seemingly more skilled and confident, was intimidating. But the supportive environment and structured nature of the classes provided a sense of security.

- **INITIAL CHALLENGES**

    The early stages were tough. Partner drills, sparring, and even the communal warm-ups triggered my anxiety. The fear of making mistakes in front of others or being judged for my lack of skill was overwhelming.

- **FINDING SUPPORT**

    The Taekwon-Do community played a crucial role in my journey. Instructors and fellow students were encouraging and non-judgmental. Their support helped me feel

TECHNIQUES FOR MANAGING SOCIAL ANXIETY IN TAEKWON-DO

Taekwon-Do offers specific techniques and practices that can help manage social anxiety. These strategies, while initially applied within the dojang, have broader applications in everyday life.

- **CONTROLLED BREATHING**

    Learning to control my breathing during intense training sessions helped manage anxiety. Slow, deep breaths can calm the nervous system and reduce physical symptoms of anxiety.

- **MINDFULNESS AND FOCUS**

    Focusing on the present moment and the task at hand, rather than worrying about others' perceptions, was a valuable lesson from Taekwon-Do. Mindfulness exercises helped shift my focus away from anxiety-inducing thoughts.

- **GRADUAL EXPOSURE**

    The progressive nature of Taekwon-Do training, where new skills are introduced gradually, allowed for step-by-step exposure to anxiety-provoking situations. This gradual exposure helped desensitize my fear of social interactions.

- **POSITIVE SELF-TALK**

    Replacing negative thoughts with positive affirmations was crucial. Encouraging myself with phrases like "I am capable" or "I can handle this" helped build confidence and reduce anxiety.

BUILDING CONFIDENCE THROUGH ACHIEVEMEN

Achieving milestones in Taekwon-Do, from mastering new techniques to progressing through belt ranks, played a significant role in building my confidence and reducing social anxiety.

- **SKILL MASTERY**

    Each new technique learned and perfected was a testament to my ability to overcome challenges. This sense of accomplishment boosted my self-esteem and confidence.

- **BELT PROGRESSION**

    Advancing through the belt ranks provided clear, tangible evidence of my progress. Each new belt represented not only improved physical skills but also growth in mental resilience and confidence.

- **PUBLIC DEMONSTRATIONS**

    Participating in belt tests and public demonstrations, though initially nerve-wracking, became opportunities to face and conquer my fears. The positive feedback and recognition from instructors and peers reinforced my self-worth.

APPLYING LESSONS BEYOND THE DOJANG

The skills and confidence gained in Taekwon-Do had a profound impact on my ability to manage social anxiety in everyday life.

- **SOCIAL INTERACTIONS**

    The confidence developed in the dojang translated into more comfortable and assertive social interactions. Meeting new people, engaging in conversations, and expressing my opinions became less daunting.

- **PROFESSIONAL SETTINGS**

    The ability to stay calm under pressure and present myself confidently improved my performance in professional settings. Public speaking and participating in meetings became manageable and even enjoyable.

- **PERSONAL RELATIONSHIPS**

    Building meaningful personal relationships, which was previously hindered by social anxiety, became more attainable. The self-assurance gained through Taekwon-Do allowed me to form deeper connections with others.

PERSONAL REFLECTIONS

TRIUMPH OVER SOCIAL ANXIETY

Reflecting on my journey, I can see how Taekwon-Do has been instrumental in transforming my life. Here are some personal reflections on the milestones and lessons learned along the way.

- **THE TURNING POINT**

    One pivotal moment was successfully completing my first belt test. The sense of accomplishment and the recognition from my instructors and peers was a turning point in my battle with social anxiety. It was a clear indication that I could face and overcome my fears.

- **CONTINUOUS GROWTH**

    The journey didn't end with a single achievement. Each class, each sparring session, and each new technique mastered was a step forward. The continuous growth in Taekwon-Do mirrored my ongoing progress in managing social anxiety.

- **A SUPPORTIVE COMMUNITY**

    The sense of belonging and support from the Taekwon-Do community cannot be overstated. The camaraderie and encouragement from fellow students and instructors provided a safe space to confront and manage my fears.

PRACTICAL EXERCISES FOR OVERCOMING SOCIAL ANXIETY

To help others facing similar challenges, here are some practical exercises and techniques that can be incorporated into Taekwon-Do practice and daily life.

- **CONTROLLED BREATHING EXERCISES**

  Practice slow, deep breathing exercises daily. Focus on inhaling deeply through the nose, holding for a few seconds, and exhaling slowly through the mouth. This can help manage anxiety symptoms in both training and social situations.

- **MINDFULNESS MEDITATION**

  Incorporate mindfulness meditation into your routine. Spend a few minutes each day focusing on your breath and being present in the moment. This practice can help reduce anxiety and improve focus.

- **GRADUAL EXPOSURE TO SOCIAL SITUATIONS**

  Start with small, manageable social interactions and gradually increase the complexity. For example, begin by making small talk with a classmate and progress to larger group interactions.

- **POSITIVE AFFIRMATIONS**

  Develop a habit of using positive affirmations. Write down encouraging statements about your abilities and repeat them daily. This can help build confidence and counteract negative self-talk.

- **VISUALISING SUCCESS**

  Before sparring sessions or social interactions, spend a few minutes visualizing a positive outcome. Imagine yourself performing confidently and successfully. This mental rehearsal can reduce anxiety and improve performance.v

CONCLUSION

THE JOURNEY CONTINUES

Overcoming social anxiety is a continuous journey, one that requires persistence, courage, and support. My experience with Taekwon-Do has shown that martial arts can be a powerful tool for managing and overcoming social fears. The skills and confidence gained through training extend far beyond the dojang, enhancing personal growth and improving quality of life.

As we continue this journey, the next chapters will delve into more advanced strategies for integrating mental and physical training, the importance of resilience, and how the principles of Taekwon-Do can be applied to various aspects of life. Join me as we explore the true potential of martial arts as a tool for personal growth, self-defense, and overcoming life's challenges.

CHAPTER 10

THE PATH FORWARD

EMBRACING THE CHALLENGE OF SPARRING

Embracing the challenge of sparring is not just about improving as a martial artist; it's about enhancing every aspect of your life. Sparring puts you under pressure, pushes your limits, and teaches you invaluable lessons about resilience, focus, and self-confidence. This chapter will delve into the multifaceted benefits of sparring, explore the rigorous training required to excel, and provide insights into creating a personalized sparring program. Additionally, I will introduce my next book on tactical sparring, designed to take your skills to the next level.

THE BENEFITS OF SPARRING

BEYOND THE DOJANG

Sparring in Taekwon-Do offers a unique opportunity to develop physical and mental skills that extend beyond martial arts. Here are some key areas where sparring can positively impact your life:

- **STRESS MANAGEMENT**

    Sparring places you in high-pressure situations where you must remain calm and focused. This ability to manage stress and stay composed under pressure translates into better stress management in everyday life, whether in the workplace, in social situations, or during personal challenges.

- **PROBLEM-SOLVING SKILLS**

    During sparring, you must think on your feet, anticipate your opponent's moves, and react quickly. This enhances your problem-solving skills, making you more adept at handling unexpected situations and finding solutions in real-time.

- **PHYSICAL FITNESS**

    Sparring is an intense workout that improves cardiovascular health, builds strength, and increases endurance. The physical benefits of sparring contribute to overall health and well-being, reducing the risk of chronic diseases and enhancing energy levels.

- **RESILIENCE AND PERSEVERANCE**

    Sparring teaches resilience by pushing you to overcome obstacles, endure setbacks, and keep striving for improvement. This resilience is essential for achieving personal and professional goals, helping you bounce back from failures and persist in the face of challenges.

- **SELF-CONFIDENCE**

    Successfully engaging in sparring builds self-confidence. The knowledge that you can face and overcome physical and mental challenges boosts your self-esteem, empowering you to tackle other areas of your life with greater confidence.

- **DISCIPLINE AND FOCUS**

    The discipline required for sparring—consistent training, adherence to techniques, and mental focus—fosters a disciplined approach to other aspects of life. Improved focus enhances productivity and helps you stay committed to your goals.

TRAINING FOR SPARRING

THE PATH TO EXCELLENCE

To excel in sparring, a structured and comprehensive training program is essential. Here's a detailed guide to the key components of effective sparring training:

- **PHYSICAL CONDITIONING**

    Cardiovascular Training: Incorporate high-intensity interval training (HIIT), running, and skipping rope to improve cardiovascular endurance.

    Strength Training: Focus on functional strength exercises such as squats, lunges, push-ups, and core workouts to build the necessary strength for powerful techniques.

    Flexibility and Mobility: Include stretching routines, yoga, and dynamic warm-ups to enhance flexibility and prevent injuries.

- **TECHNICAL SKILLS**

    Basics and Fundamentals: Regularly practice fundamental techniques such as punches, kicks, blocks, and stances. Precision in basics is crucial for advanced sparring.

    Combination Drills: Work on combinations of techniques to develop fluidity and adaptability. Practice moving seamlessly between offensive and defensive moves.

    Footwork and Movement: Train your footwork to improve agility, balance, and positioning. Practice moving in and out of range, pivoting, and maintaining proper stance.

- **SPARRING DRILLS**

    Partner Drills: Engage in controlled sparring drills with a partner to practice timing, distance, and reaction. Focus on specific scenarios such as counterattacks, defensive maneuvers, and offensive combinations.

    Shadow Sparring: Visualize an opponent and practice sparring techniques alone. This helps improve muscle memory and mental preparation.

    Live Sparring: Participate in live sparring sessions to simulate real competition conditions. Vary the intensity and focus on applying techniques learned in training.

- **MENTAL TRAINING**

    Visualization: Regularly visualize sparring scenarios, including successful techniques and strategies. Visualization enhances mental preparation and confidence.

Mindfulness and Focus: Practice mindfulness exercises and meditation to improve focus and mental clarity. This helps in maintaining composure during high-pressure sparring.

Positive Self-Talk: Develop a habit of positive self-talk to boost confidence and reduce anxiety. Encourage yourself with affirmations and focus on your strengths.

- **STRATEGY AND TACTICS**

    Opponent Analysis: Study different sparring styles and strategies. Understand your opponent's strengths and weaknesses to develop effective counter-strategies.

    Adaptability: Practice adapting to different opponents and situations. Flexibility in strategy is crucial for success in sparring.

    Game Plan Development: Create a game plan for sparring sessions, focusing on specific techniques, combinations, and strategies you want to implement.

CREATING A PERSONALISED SPARRING PROGRAM

For those interested in developing their sparring skills, I offer personalized sparring programs. Contact me through my social media platforms to discuss your goals, current skill level, and training preferences. Here's an outline of what a personalized program might include:

- **ASSESSMENT AND GOAL SETTING**

    Initial assessment of your current fitness level, technical skills, and sparring experience. Define specific short-term and long-term goals for your sparring development.

- **CUSTOMIZED TRAINING PLAN**

    Physical Conditioning: Tailored workouts to improve strength, endurance, and flexibility based on your fitness level.

    Technical Skills: Drills and exercises focused on enhancing your specific techniques and combinations.

    Sparring Drills: Structured sparring sessions with progression from controlled drills to live sparring.

    Mental Training: Techniques to improve focus, visualization practices, and strategies for managing sparring anxiety.

- **REGULAR PROGRESS REVIEWS**

    Periodic assessments to monitor progress and adjust the training plan as needed. Feedback and guidance to help you stay on track and achieve your goals.

- **SUPPORT AND MOTIVATION**

    Ongoing support and motivation to keep you engaged and committed to your training. Tips and advice for maintaining a balanced approach to training and avoiding burn out.

TOOLS AND RESOURCES

To support your sparring journey, I recommend the following tools and resources:

- **TRAINING EQUIPMENT**

    Invest in quality training gear, including gloves, pads, protective gear, and a jump rope for conditioning.

- **TRAINING JOURNAL**

    Keep a training journal to track your progress, note techniques and combinations, and reflect on sparring sessions.

- **ONLINE RESOURCES**

    Periodic assessments to monitor progress and adjust the training plan as needed. Feedback and guidance to help you stay on track and achieve your goals.

- **SUPPORT AND MOTIVATION**

    Utilse online platforms for additional training videos, tutorials, and community support. Websites and social media groups dedicated to Taekwon-Do can provide valuable insights and inspiration.

- **BOOKS AND ARTICLES**

    Read books and articles on martial arts, sparring strategies, and mental training to deepen your knowledge and understanding.